I0425872

March 2012

NURSING HOMES

CMS Needs Milestones and Timelines to Ensure Goals for the Five-Star Quality Rating System Are Met

G A O
Accountability ★ Integrity ★ Reliability

GAO-12-390

March 2012

NURSING HOMES

CMS Needs Milestones and Timelines to Ensure Goals for the Five-Star Quality Rating System Are Met

Why GAO Did This Study

In 2008, in an effort to provide helpful information to consumers and improve provider quality, the Centers for Medicare & Medicaid Services (CMS) developed and implemented the Five-Star Quality Rating System (Five-Star System). The Five-Star System assigns each nursing home an overall rating and three component ratings—health inspections, staffing, and quality measures—based on the extent to which the nursing home meets CMS's quality standards and other measures. The rating scale ranges from one to five stars, with more stars indicating higher quality.

The Patient Protection and Affordable Care Act directed GAO to review CMS's Five-Star System. This report examines (1) how CMS developed and implemented the Five-Star System and what key methodological decisions were made during development, (2) the circumstances under which CMS considers modifying the Five-Star System, and (3) the extent to which CMS has established plans to help ensure it achieves its goals for the Five-Star System. To conduct this work, GAO reviewed CMS documents, interviewed CMS officials and others, and assessed whether CMS uses certain strategic planning practices.

What GAO Recommends

GAO recommends that the Administrator of CMS use strategic planning to establish how its planned efforts will help meet the goals of the Five-Star System, and develop milestones and timelines for each of its planned efforts. CMS agreed with these recommendations.

View GAO-12-390. For more information, contact Linda Kohn at (202) 512-7114 or kohnl@gao.gov.

What GAO Found

CMS developed and implemented the Five-Star System largely during an 8-month period in 2008 with input from long-term care stakeholders, CMS's Five-Star System contractor, and members of a technical expert panel—a panel composed of nine individuals that CMS identified as experts in long-term care research. CMS made numerous methodological decisions during the development of the Five-Star System, including three key methodological decisions. GAO defines key methodological decisions as those that at least six technical expert panel members—of the nine that GAO contacted—recalled as eliciting the most intense review and discussion during the development of the Five-Star System. One key methodological decision was how to combine the component ratings to create an overall rating. The other two key methodological decisions pertained to how to create ratings that account for variation in the type of care provided across nursing homes.

CMS generally considers modifying the Five-Star System in response to (1) methodological issues raised by stakeholders, (2) its routine monitoring of the system, and (3) the availability of new data sources. CMS officials explained that when a methodological issue is raised by long-term care stakeholders, they review the Five-Star System to determine whether modifications should be made. Officials said that each issue raised does not always result in modifications to the Five-Star System, although some minor modifications have been made. CMS also considers making modifications to the Five-Star System based on its periodic analyses of trends of the system; however, to date, no modifications have been made based on these analyses. Lastly, CMS is currently determining how to modify the staffing and quality measure ratings of the Five-Star System based on newly available data.

CMS has several planned efforts intended to improve the Five-Star System, including evaluating the usability of the system, adding nursing home capability information, revising the staffing component, and developing additional quality measures. However, CMS lacks GAO-identified leading strategic planning practices—the use of milestones and timelines to guide and gauge progress toward achieving desired results and the alignment of activities, resources, and goals—that could help the agency to more efficiently and effectively accomplish its planned efforts intended to improve the Five-Star System. While CMS officials have given us broad estimates for when they anticipate some of these efforts to be implemented, CMS does not have milestones and timelines associated with implementing the efforts, which could help ensure that appropriate progress is made towards implementation. In addition, CMS has not established, through planning documents, how its planned efforts to improve the Five-Star System will help CMS achieve the goals of the system—to inform consumers and improve provider quality. As a result, CMS may not be identifying and prioritizing its intended improvements in a manner that best ensures that the goals are being achieved.

Contents

Figures

Abbreviations

AHRQ	Agency for Healthcare Research and Quality
CMS	Centers for Medicare & Medicaid Services
GPRA	Government Performance and Results Act
HHS	Department of Health and Human Services
MDS	Minimum Data Set
RN	registered nurse
RUG	Resource Utilization Group

GAO
Accountability * Integrity * Reliability

United States Government Accountability Office
Washington, DC 20548

March 23, 2012

The Honorable Max Baucus
Chairman
The Honorable Orin Hatch
Ranking Member
Committee on Finance
United States Senate

The Honorable Fred Upton
Chairman
The Honorable Henry Waxman
Ranking Member
Committee on Energy and Commerce
House of Representatives

The Honorable Dave Camp
Chairman
The Honorable Sander Levin
Ranking Member
Committee on Ways and Means
House of Representatives

The nation's almost 3.3 million nursing home residents are a vulnerable population of elderly and disabled individuals who rely on nursing homes to provide high-quality care. In 2009, these nursing home consumers and their families had about 15,900 nursing homes participating in the Medicare and Medicaid programs from which to choose for their care needs.[1] When deciding on a nursing home, consumers and their families can make choices based on such factors as location, fees, specialties, services and activities for residents, and what they know about the quality of care provided in a facility. The Centers for Medicare & Medicaid Services (CMS), an agency within the Department of Health and Human Services (HHS), is responsible for establishing quality standards that nursing homes must meet in the delivery of care to their residents and for

---

[1]Medicare is the federal health insurance program for persons aged 65 or over, certain disabled individuals, and individuals with end-stage renal disease. Medicaid is the joint federal-state health care financing program for certain categories of low-income individuals.

overseeing nursing homes' compliance with those standards. In our prior work, we have shown that the quality of care provided in nursing homes can vary, often significantly, and have raised concerns about the quality of care in some nursing homes. For example, our prior reports have found that some nursing homes have been cited repeatedly for serious deficiencies, such as residents having preventable pressure ulcers that harmed them or put them at risk of death or serious injury.[2]

Given the various factors nursing home consumers may consider when choosing a facility, including quality of care, the variability in the quality of care provided across nursing homes, and concerns over quality of care problems in some nursing homes, CMS has taken steps to provide assistance to individuals and their families in choosing a nursing home. Specifically, in 1998 CMS began publicly reporting information related to the quality of nursing homes on its *Nursing Home Compare* website.[3] However, in 2007, some members of Congress raised concerns that this information was not helpful to consumers because it was difficult to understand.

To address these concerns, in 2008 CMS developed and implemented the Nursing Home Five-Star Quality Rating System (Five-Star System), which is posted on the *Nursing Home Compare* website. The primary goal of the Five-Star System is to help consumers make informed decisions about their care by providing understandable and useful information on nursing home quality. The secondary goal of the Five-Star System is to help improve nursing home quality by publicly reporting quality of care information, as some research has suggested that publishing such information can create an incentive for providers to improve their quality of care. The Five-Star System assigns each nursing home an overall rating and three component ratings based on the extent to which the nursing home meets CMS's quality standards and other measures. The rating scale ranges from one to five stars, with more stars indicating higher quality.

---

[2]See GAO, *Nursing Homes: Addressing the Factors Underlying Understatement of Serious Care Problems Requires Sustained CMS and State Commitment,* GAO-10-70 (Washington, D.C.: Nov. 24, 2009), and *Poorly Performing Nursing Homes: Special Focus Facilities Are Often Improving, but CMS's Program Could Be Strengthened,* GAO-10-197 (Washington, D.C.: Mar. 19, 2010).

[3]www.Medicare.gov/NHCompare/home.asp.

Some long-term care stakeholders have voiced support for the Five-Star System, stating that it helps consumers choose a nursing home for themselves or a family member.[4] However, other long-term care stakeholders and some members of Congress have raised questions about the Five-Star System, such as how the system was developed and implemented and whether CMS is taking steps to make the system more useful to consumers. For example, provider advocacy groups have raised questions about the methodology used to develop the ratings and consumer advocacy groups have made suggestions on the substance and presentation of the Five-Star System in an effort to improve the information provided to consumers.

The Patient Protection and Affordable Care Act directed us to review CMS's Five-Star System.[5] This report examines (1) how CMS developed and implemented the Five-Star System and what key methodological decisions were made during development, (2) the circumstances under which CMS considers modifying the Five-Star System, and (3) the extent to which CMS has established plans to help ensure it achieves its goals for the Five-Star System.

To describe how CMS developed and implemented the Five-Star System, including the key methodological decisions that CMS made during development, we interviewed senior CMS officials responsible for the system about the development and implementation of the system. We reviewed documents from CMS and its Five-Star System contractor—the contractor to which CMS awarded a contract to assist with development and implementation of the system.[6] These documents include those describing how CMS communicated information about the Five-Star System to individuals and entities outside of CMS, meetings CMS's contractor convened with a panel of nine individuals that CMS and its contractor identified as experts in long-term care research—referred to in this report as the "technical expert panel"—to solicit and discuss potential approaches to calculate nursing home ratings, and the methodology used

---

[4]Long-term care stakeholders include nursing home providers, consumers, and advocacy groups that represent consumers or providers.

[5]Pub. L. No. 111-148, § 6107, 124 Stat. 119, 713 (2010).

[6]The CMS Five-Star System contractor is a consulting firm that employs health services researchers and other support staff and conducts research in a range of fields, including health care policy.

to calculate the ratings, including the reasoning behind CMS's final methodological decisions. Finally, we identified the key methodological decisions—which we define as the methodological decisions that at least six of the members of the technical expert panel recalled as eliciting the most intense discussion and review during development of the Five-Star System—using a series of interviews and questionnaires. We interviewed all nine technical expert panel members and received responses to our questionnaire from seven of the nine members. For additional information on our approach to identify the key methodological decisions, see appendix I.

To describe the circumstances under which CMS considers modifying the Five-Star System, we interviewed senior CMS officials about the factors that prompt CMS to examine potential modifications to the system. We also reviewed documents describing modifications made to the Five-Star System since its implementation in December 2008 and the reasons those modifications were made. In addition, we reviewed analyses of the Five-Star System's rating results that CMS's Five-Star System contractor has been conducting since the system's implementation in December 2008.

To describe the extent to which CMS has established plans to help ensure it achieves its goals for the Five-Star System, we interviewed CMS officials, including senior officials responsible for the Five-Star System, those involved in strategic planning for the agency, and those involved in displaying health care information for consumers on CMS's websites. We identified and reviewed documents related to CMS's plans for improving the Five-Star System as well as documents that relate to the system's goals—informing consumers and improving provider quality. We interviewed officials and reviewed documents from the HHS Agency for Healthcare Research and Quality (AHRQ) regarding best practices AHRQ has identified for effectively displaying health care quality information to consumers on websites. Since the mid-1990s, we have identified a variety of leading practices for effective strategic planning in accordance with the Government Performance and Results Act

(GPRA).[7,8] We assessed whether CMS's plans for improving the Five-Star System and achieving its goals include two GAO-identified leading practices for successful strategic planning and management: (1) using intermediate goals and measures to show progress or contribution to intended results, and (2) aligning activities and resources to support agency goals.

We conducted this performance audit from June 2011 through March 2012 in accordance with generally accepted government auditing standards. Those standards require that we plan and perform the audit to obtain sufficient, appropriate evidence to provide a reasonable basis for our findings and conclusions based on our audit objectives. We believe that the evidence obtained provides a reasonable basis for our findings and conclusions based on our audit objectives.

Background

CMS has publicly reported information on nursing home quality on its *Nursing Home Compare* website since 1998 and has increased the amount of information it reports on the website over time.[9] On June 18, 2008, CMS announced its plans to make use of the information available on the *Nursing Home Compare* website and begin assigning each nursing home "star" ratings to help beneficiaries, their families, and caregivers compare nursing homes more easily. Beginning in December 2008, CMS made the Five-Star System publicly available on its *Nursing Home Compare* website. The Five-Star System assigns star ratings for each nursing home participating in the Medicare and/or Medicaid programs.

---

[7]GAO, *Managing for Results: Enhancing Agency Use of Performance Information for Management Decision Making*, GAO-05-927 (Washington, D.C.: Sept. 9, 2005); *Agency Performance Plans: Examples of Practices That Can Improve Usefulness to Decisionmakers*, GAO/GGD/AIMD-99-69 (Washington, D.C.: Feb. 26, 1999); *Agencies' Strategic Plans Under GPRA: Key Questions to Facilitate Congressional Review*, GAO/GGD-10.1.16 (Washington, D.C.: May 1997); *Managing for Results: Critical Issues for Improving Federal Agencies' Strategic Plans*, GAO/GGD-97-180 (Washington, D.C.: Sept. 16, 1997); and *Executive Guide: Effectively Implementing the Government Performance and Results Act*, GAO/GGD-96-118 (Washington, D.C.: June 1996).

[8]Government Performance and Results Act of 1993, Pub. L. No. 103-62, 107 Stat. 285 (1993) and the GPRA Modernization Act of 2010, Pub. L. No. 111-352, 124 Stat. 3866 (2011).

[9]CMS initially reported information about nursing home characteristics and survey results on its *Nursing Home Compare* website. Later, CMS began reporting additional information, such as the ratio of nursing staff to residents.

These star ratings include a separate rating for each of the three components—health inspections, staffing, and quality measures—in addition to an overall rating.[10]

- **Health inspection rating**. CMS contracts with state survey agencies to conduct unannounced, on-site nursing home health inspections—known as surveys—to determine whether nursing homes meet federal quality standards. Every nursing home receiving Medicare or Medicaid payment must undergo a standard survey not less than once every 15 months, and the statewide average interval for these surveys must not exceed 12 months.[11] State surveyors also conduct complaint investigations in response to allegations of quality problems. State surveyors may spend several days in the nursing home to assess whether the nursing home is in compliance with federal quality standards. If nursing homes are found to be out of compliance with any requirements, state surveyors issue deficiency citations that reflect the scope (number of residents affected) and severity (level of harm to residents) of the deficiency. The health inspection rating is a result of nursing home performance on surveys and complaint investigations.[12]

  Specifically, this star rating is based on the scope and severity of deficiencies from the last 3 years of routine surveys and complaint investigations. To calculate this rating, the most recent survey findings are weighted more heavily than those from the prior 2 years. A nursing home's health inspection rating is relative to other nursing homes' health inspection ratings in their state. This rating is updated for each nursing home when new survey data become available for that facility.

---

[10]Some nursing homes may have fewer than four ratings because CMS does not assign a rating if certain criteria established by CMS are not met, such as reporting reliable data.

[11]See 42 U.S.C. §§ 1395i-3(g)(2)(A)(iii), 1396r(g)(2)(A)(iii).

[12]CMS started posting the results of surveys on *Nursing Home Compare* in 1998. According to CMS, the strengths of the surveys are that they are conducted by trained individuals and follow national standards. Also, according to CMS, limitations of these surveys are that the data are only collected about one time a year and deficiency citations are subject to the interpretation of the trained state surveyor.

- **Staffing rating**. Nursing homes self-report staffing hours for a 2-week period at the time of the routine survey. CMS converts the reported point-in-time staffing hours for nursing staff—registered nurses, licensed practical nurses, and certified nursing assistants—into measures that indicate the number of registered nurse and total nursing hours per resident per day.[13]

  This star rating is based on the reported registered nurse and total nursing staffing levels, adjusted for differences in the level of complexity of nursing services required to care for residents across nursing homes—referred to as resident acuity. The adjustment for resident acuity is done using data from a resident assessment tool called the Minimum Data Set (MDS), which nursing homes complete and periodically report to CMS. MDS collects information on residents' health, physical functioning, mental status, and general well-being.[14] Each nursing home's staffing rating is assigned based on how its total nursing and registered nurse staffing levels compare to the distribution of staffing levels for freestanding facilities[15] in the nation and staffing level thresholds identified by CMS.[16] In addition, this rating is updated when new staffing data are collected at the time of the routine survey, generally every 12 months.

---

[13]Total nursing hours are the sum of registered and licensed practical nurse and certified nursing assistant hours. In 2000, CMS began publicly reporting information on nursing home staffing levels on *Nursing Home Compare*. According to CMS, the strength of staffing data is that there is a relationship between staffing and quality of care and that staffing data collected by CMS are understandable for the consumer. In addition, according to CMS, a limitation of these data is that they are self-reported by nursing home staff about one time per year.

[14]CMS measures resident acuity using the Resource Utilization Group (RUG)-III case mix system that uses resident assessment data routinely collected in MDS. This system classifies residents into 1 of 53 categories according to predicted resource needs, particularly the expected amount of staff time required to care for residents. In October 2010, CMS implemented a new version of MDS—MDS 3.0—and this will change the data used for the case mix system.

[15]Freestanding nursing homes are those that are not under administrative control of a hospital.

[16]See AM Kramer and R. Fish, Abt Associates, "The Relationship Between Nurse Staffing Levels and the Quality of Nursing Home Care," chapter 2 in *Appropriateness of Minimum Nurse Staffing Ratios in Nursing Homes: Phase II Final Report,* a report prepared at the request of CMS (2001).

- **Quality measure rating**. CMS uses data from MDS to calculate various quality measures for each nursing home. These measures include, for example, the prevalence of pressure sores and changes in residents' mobility.[17]

  This star rating is based on 10 different quality measures. This rating is typically updated quarterly. Quality measure ratings are assigned to generally achieve the following distribution: the top 10 percent of nursing homes receive five stars, the bottom 20 percent receive one star, and the middle 70 percent of nursing homes receive two, three, or four stars, with equal proportions (23.33 percent) in each category.[18] However, CMS has not updated the quality measure ratings since January 2011 to allow CMS to collect resident information from nursing homes using a new version of MDS and refine and test quality measures using this revised assessment tool.

The overall star rating is calculated using a process that combines the star ratings from the health inspection, staffing, and quality measure components. The overall rating is assigned based on the following steps:

1. Start with the number of stars for the health inspection rating.

2. Add one star if the staffing rating is four or five stars and also greater than the health inspection rating. Subtract one star if the staffing rating is one star. The rating cannot go above five stars or lower than one star.

---

[17]In 2002, CMS began posting nursing homes' quality measures on *Nursing Home Compare*. According to CMS, the strengths of the quality measures are that they are an in-depth look at key aspects of care and are validated through a formal process. In addition, CMS notes that limitations of the quality measures are that the data for these measures are self-reported by nursing home staff and that quality measures are narrowly focused on specific aspects of quality of care.

[18]Performance on the two activities of daily living-related measures is weighted 1.6667 times as high as the other measures. In addition, thresholds for the two activities of daily living quality measures are reset with each quarterly update of the quality measures data based on the state-specific distribution of these measures. Thresholds for the other quality measure ratings are fixed based on the national distribution of these measures on January 5, 2009.

3. Add one star if the quality measure rating is five stars. Subtract one star if the quality measure rating is one star. The rating cannot go above five stars or lower than one star.[19]

See figure 1 for an example of how a nursing home's overall rating is calculated. This rating is updated when any of the three component ratings change. For example, changes to the quality measure rating could change a nursing home's overall rating.

---

[19]The overall rating is capped in two circumstances. First, if a nursing home's health inspection rating is one star, then the overall rating cannot exceed two stars. Second, nursing homes currently in the Special Focus Facility Program— a program that aims to remedy noncompliance with federal quality standards in nursing homes with repeated cycles of noncompliance with these standards—have their overall rating capped at three stars even if they have high ratings in individual components.

Figure 1: Calculating the Overall Rating for the Five-Star System

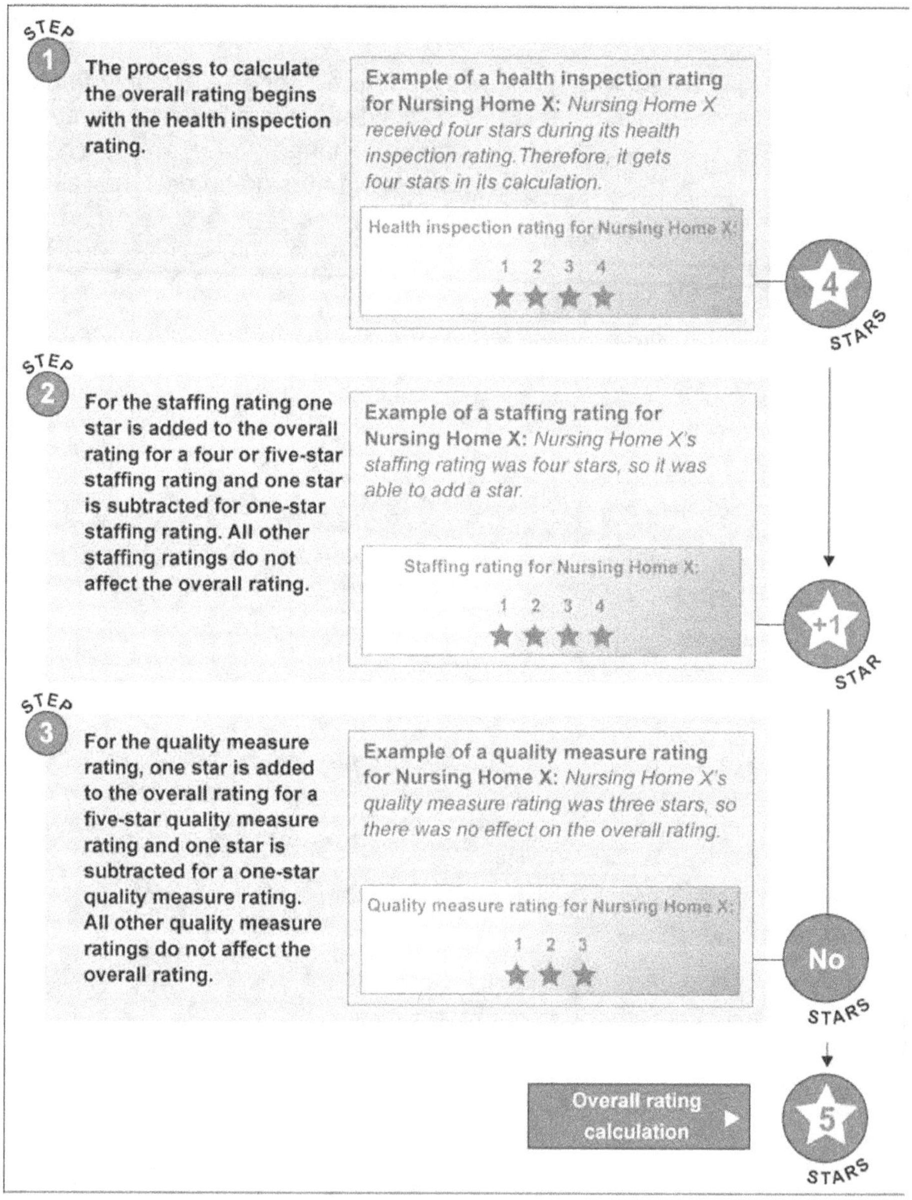

STEP 1

The process to calculate the overall rating begins with the health inspection rating.

Example of a health inspection rating for Nursing Home X: *Nursing Home X received four stars during its health inspection rating. Therefore, it gets four stars in its calculation.*

Health inspection rating for Nursing Home X:

1 2 3 4

★ ★ ★ ★

4 STARS

STEP 2

For the staffing rating one star is added to the overall rating for a four or five-star staffing rating and one star is subtracted for one-star staffing rating. All other staffing ratings do not affect the overall rating.

Example of a staffing rating for Nursing Home X: *Nursing Home X's staffing rating was four stars, so it was able to add a star.*

Staffing rating for Nursing Home X:

1 2 3 4

★ ★ ★ ★

+1 STAR

STEP 3

For the quality measure rating, one star is added to the overall rating for a five-star quality measure rating and one star is subtracted for a one-star quality measure rating. All other quality measure ratings do not affect the overall rating.

Example of a quality measure rating for Nursing Home X: *Nursing Home X's quality measure rating was three stars, so there was no effect on the overall rating.*

Quality measure rating for Nursing Home X:

1 2 3

★ ★ ★

No STARS

Overall rating calculation ▶

5 STARS

Source: GAO analysis of CMS information.

See appendix II for additional information on the methodology for calculating nursing home ratings under the Five-Star System.

CMS Used Input from External Entities on the Development and Implementation of the Five-Star System, Which Included Three Key Methodological Decisions

CMS developed and implemented the Five-Star System largely during an 8-month period with input from long-term care stakeholders, its Five-Star System contractor, and members of a technical expert panel. CMS made numerous methodological decisions during the development of the Five-Star System, including three key methodological decisions that elicited the most discussion during development.

CMS Solicited Input from Long-term Care Stakeholders, a Contractor, and a Panel of Experts

CMS largely developed and implemented the Five-Star System during an 8-month period from April to December 2008, soliciting input from long-term care stakeholders, the Five-Star System contractor, and members of a technical expert panel. For example, after the Acting Administrator of CMS directed CMS officials to develop a rating system for nursing homes in late April 2008, CMS obtained comments about the planned rating system from long-term care stakeholders through an Open Door Forum[20] in June 2008. CMS also reviewed and summarized comments it received via an email account set up specifically for comments regarding the planned rating system through late July.[21] Concurrently, CMS developed the methodology to calculate nursing home ratings in collaboration with the Five-Star System contractor and members of a technical expert panel. CMS's contractor established this panel, composed of nine members that the contractor and CMS identified as experts in long-term care and that included researchers and an industry representative, to help guide the development and implementation of the Five-Star System.[22] CMS and its contractor convened five meetings with the technical expert panel between July and December 2008 to review and discuss analyses

---

[20]CMS convenes Open Door Forums to provide an opportunity for dialogue between CMS and the provider community and others to help them to understand contemporary program issues, such as the development of new rating systems.

[21]CMS summarized comments it received on the Five-Star System through July 23, 2008. CMS continued to receive comments on the Five-Star System via email (BetterCare@cms.hhs.gov) after July 23, 2008, though those comments were not included in CMS's summary of comments on the system.

[22]For a list of the current technical expert panel members, see https://www.cms.gov/CertificationandComplianc/13_FSQRS.asp.

conducted by the Five-Star System contractor regarding various options for calculating the ratings. In November and December 2008, CMS hosted meetings with reporters and other government entities, including the HHS Administration on Aging, and hosted another Open Door Forum to discuss the impending implementation of the Five-Star System with stakeholders. In December 2008, CMS gave nursing home providers a preview of their ratings and, on December 18, 2008, CMS made the Five-Star System publicly available on the *Nursing Home Compare* website. (See fig. 2 for a timeline of CMS's development and implementation of the Five-Star System.)

Figure 2: Timeline of Development and Implementation of the Five-Star System, April to December 2008

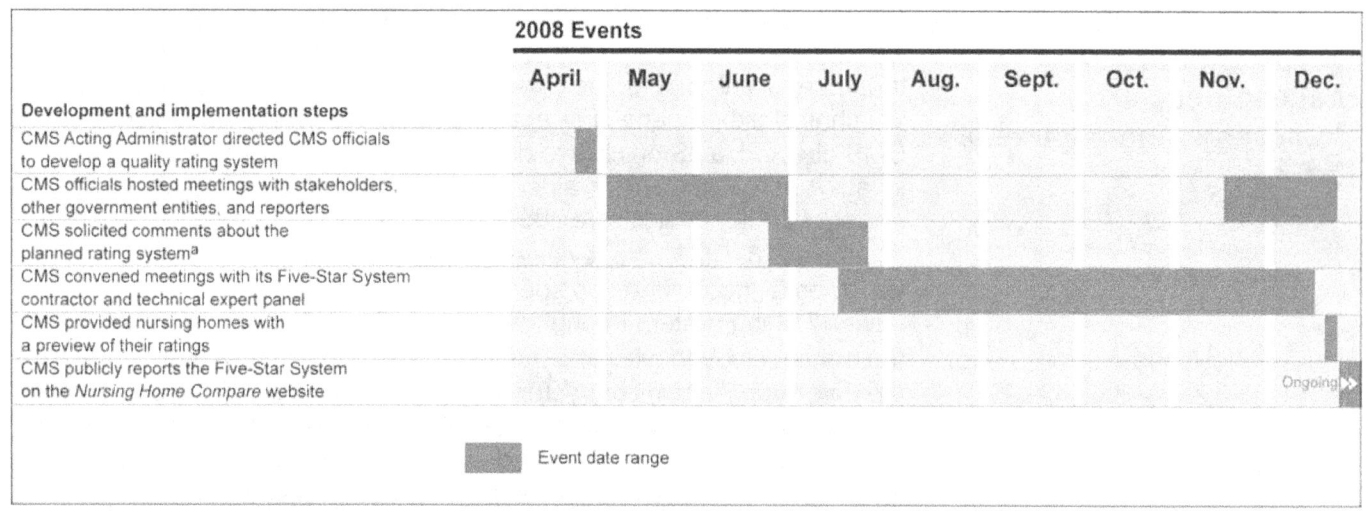

Source: GAO analysis of CMS information.

[a]CMS continued to receive comments on the Five-Star System via email after July 2008, though those comments were not included in CMS's summary of comments on the system.

Three Key Methodological Decisions Elicited the Most Discussion during Development

CMS made numerous methodological decisions during the development of the Five-Star System, including three key methodological decisions. We define key methodological decisions as those that at least six members of CMS's technical expert panel recalled as eliciting the most intense review and discussion during the development of the Five-Star

System.[23] According to the panel experts, one key methodological decision was how to combine the component ratings to create an overall rating. The other two key methodological decisions pertain to how to create ratings that account for variation in the type of care provided across nursing homes. Specifically, the second key methodological decision the experts recalled was whether to exclude hospital-based nursing homes or set up separate ratings for hospital-based and freestanding nursing homes.[24] The third key methodological decision the experts recalled was whether the staffing rating should be based on nursing staffing levels that are adjusted to reflect resident acuity.

- **How to combine the component ratings to create an overall rating.** One key methodological decision that CMS made was deciding how to best combine the health inspection, quality measure, and staffing component ratings to create an overall rating. Technical expert panel members told us that they discussed how much weight should be assigned to each component when combining the component ratings to calculate the overall rating. One technical expert panel member told us that, in the end, the members generally agreed to assign more weight to the health inspection and staffing components and less weight to the quality measure component, which reflects differences in the perceived validity and reliability of the data used to calculate these components. Consistent with the technical expert panel's proposal, CMS decided to assign overall ratings to each nursing home by starting with the health inspection rating, then adding or subtracting stars if the nursing home's staffing or quality measure rating was particularly high or low, with a minimum and maximum rating of one and five stars, respectively.[25]

---

[23]For an overview of our approach to identify the key methodological decisions CMS made during the development of the Five-Star System, which includes a list of other methodological decisions that technical expert panel members identified as eliciting intense review and discussion, see appendix I.

[24]Hospital-based nursing homes are under administrative control of a hospital. In contrast, freestanding nursing homes are those that are not under administrative control of a hospital.

[25]Nursing homes with a one star health inspection rating cannot be upgraded by more than one star based on the staffing and quality measure ratings. In addition, nursing homes that are enrolled in CMS's Special Focus Facility Program are identified as such on the website and have a maximum overall rating of three stars. For additional information about the methodology to calculate the overall rating, see appendix II.

- **Whether to exclude hospital-based nursing homes or set up separate ratings for hospital-based and freestanding nursing homes**. Another key methodological decision that CMS made was whether to exclude nursing homes that are hospital-based from the Five-Star System or to set up separate ratings for hospital-based and freestanding nursing homes. CMS's Five-Star System contractor stated that hospital-based facilities may typically provide a different type of care than freestanding facilities. That is, hospital-based facilities may provide care to more acute residents who require more extensive services than freestanding facilities. However, one senior CMS official told us that some hospital-based and freestanding facilities may provide care to similar types of residents. While CMS considered creating separate ratings for hospital-based and freestanding nursing homes, CMS ultimately decided not to exclude hospital-based nursing homes or create a separate rating scale for hospital-based and freestanding nursing homes.

- **Whether staffing ratings should be based on nursing staffing levels that are adjusted to reflect resident acuity**. A third key methodological decision that CMS made was whether the staffing rating that nursing homes receive should be based on reported staffing levels that are adjusted to account for resident acuity. For example, in a published article, two of the technical expert panel members and others argued that the appropriate level of nurse staffing may differ substantially in two nursing homes with identical numbers of staff, because of the differences in the amount of time needed to care for residents due to variation in resident acuity.[26] However, panel members told us that they debated whether and the extent to which nursing staffing levels should be adjusted to reflect resident acuity due to concerns about the validity of existing adjustment approaches. Because CMS agreed that nursing home staffing levels should reflect the care needs of the facility's residents, CMS decided to adjust staffing levels for differences in the expected

---

[26]See C. Harrington, C. Kovner, M. Mezey, J. Kayser-Jones, S. Burger, M. Mohler, R. Burke, and D. Zimmerman, "Experts Recommend Minimum Nurse Staffing Standards for Nursing Facilities in the United States," *The Gerontologist*, vol. 40, no. 1 (2000), 5-16.

amount of time required to care for residents and worked with the technical expert panel to select an adjustment method.[27]

CMS Typically Considers Modifying the Five-Star System in Response to Stakeholders, after Routine Monitoring, and When New Data Sources Become Available

CMS generally considers modifying the Five-Star System in response to (1) methodological issues raised by stakeholders, (2) its routine monitoring of the system, and (3) the availability of new data sources. CMS officials explained that when a methodological issue is raised by long-term care stakeholders, they review the Five-Star System to determine whether modifications should be made.[28] Officials further said that each issue raised does not always result in modifications to the Five-Star System, although some minor modifications have been made. For example, in September 2009, in response to input it received from long-term care stakeholders, CMS updated the methodology for calculating a nursing home's health inspection rating. With the methodological change, the health inspection rating for a nursing home is no longer updated unless new survey data for that nursing home becomes available. Initially, because each nursing home's health inspection rating is relative to the ratings of all nursing homes in the same state, the results of new surveys and rating changes for some nursing homes could have affected the ratings for other nursing homes in the state. Stakeholders had noted to CMS that the rating of an individual nursing home therefore could be changed even if that nursing home had not had a new survey. CMS made the methodological change to address this concern, while noting that this had happened to only a small percentage of nursing homes.

Some issues raised by stakeholders have not resulted in a modification of the Five-Star System. For example, one stakeholder raised a concern that surveys should have fixed thresholds instead of thresholds that are relative to—or based on—other nursing homes' survey scores in the same state. CMS reviewed this concern with its Five-Star System contractor and found that fixed thresholds would likely present disadvantages to nursing homes because changes in survey policy could

---

[27]CMS measures resident acuity using the Resource Utilization Group (RUG)-III case mix system. This system classifies residents into 1 of 53 categories according to predicted resource needs, particularly the expected amount of staff time required to care for residents, using resident assessment data that are routinely collected by CMS from nursing homes.

[28]A senior CMS official told us that while they do not track each issue that has been raised, they write internal memorandums for issues that were raised that outline the reasoning behind whether modifications were or were not made to the Five-Star System.

lead to changes in survey scores and result in significant changes for nursing homes' health inspection ratings.[29] CMS officials stated that using a relative distribution allows nursing homes' ratings to remain more stable and, additionally, allows consumers to compare nursing homes within a state.

CMS also considers making modifications to the Five-Star System based on its periodic analysis of the system's rating trends; however, to date, no modifications have been made based on these analyses. CMS's Five-Star System contractor conducts this analysis and provides monthly reports to CMS as well as an annual report that describes changes over time in nursing homes' ratings and trend information on the individual components of the system.[30] These routine monitoring reports are intended to help CMS evaluate the Five-Star System and determine if modifications are needed. For example, CMS examined whether it should modify the health inspection component because some state survey agencies have begun using the Quality Indicator Survey to collect survey information.[31] In 2010, as part of its analysis for one of its monthly reports, CMS examined whether the health inspection rating of facilities that were inspected using the Quality Indicator Survey differed from those that were inspected with the traditional, paper-based survey. No significant difference was found between the two approaches to conducting the survey and, as a result, CMS did not modify the Five-Star System.

Lastly, CMS is currently considering how to modify the Five-Star System because new data sources have become available. Specifically, CMS is determining, with input from its Five-Star System contractor and the technical expert panel, how to modify the staffing and quality measure

---

[29]CMS conducted a retrospective analysis of health inspection ratings from 2003 through 2008 and found that the scores of nursing homes would have declined during this period if a Five-Star System with fixed thresholds had been in place.

[30]Through this analysis, CMS has found that nursing homes' star ratings have improved in the first 2 years since the Five-Star System has been implemented, but it is unclear if the results are due to more accurate reporting of the data or an actual improvement in quality.

[31]The Quality Indicator Survey is an electronic process to conduct surveys that began in 2005. As of November 2011, the implementation of the Quality Indicator Survey had been postponed in an effort to address concerns that have been raised about this new process. For more information about GAO's work on the Quality Indicator Survey, see *Nursing Home Quality: CMS Should Improve Efforts to Monitor Implementation of the Quality Indicator Survey,* GAO-12-214 (Washington, D.C.: Feb. 1, 2012).

ratings of the Five-Star System based on new data available from MDS 3.0, an updated version of the resident assessment tool. CMS is examining how using data from MDS 3.0 to adjust staffing data to account for resident acuity will affect the staffing ratings of nursing homes. In addition, CMS is considering whether the availability of these new data should result in a modification to the manner in which the thresholds for the staffing component ratings are determined. CMS intends to complete any modifications to the staffing component rating based on the new data by April 2012. CMS is also currently refining and testing the nursing home quality measures using MDS 3.0 data and is considering options for modifying how the quality measure component rating for the Five-Star System will be calculated using these new data. CMS anticipates that the quality measure component of the Five-Star System will be modified at the end of calendar year 2012. Because of these changes, CMS has not updated the Five-Star System quality measure ratings for individual nursing homes since January 2011—the last time period for which data using the previous assessment tool were available.

Similarly, CMS is considering modifying the data it uses to calculate the nursing home staffing rating based on another new data source—electronic payroll data. Although CMS currently calculates this rating based on staffing data from a 2-week period of time, CMS plans to use payroll records of nursing homes to collect staffing data from nursing homes, once these data are available in the next 3 to 5 years. A CMS official told us that the agency has determined what type of data it wants to collect through nursing home payroll systems, such as data that will allow the calculation of nursing staff turnover in a nursing home, and is working with a private firm to develop the system to collect this information. Electronic payroll data have several strengths, including that they will allow CMS to collect data on several aspects of staffing that are not currently available, including the percentage of staff that are full time and the number of staff that provide direct patient care. In addition, because payroll data originate from employees and are used to pay their salaries, CMS officials stated that they have greater confidence in the accuracy of the data. According to one senior official, CMS does not expect to determine potential modifications to the nursing home staffing rating of the Five-Star System until it has experience collecting payroll data.

Although CMS Intends to Make Improvements, the Agency Has Not Ensured That Its Efforts Will Help Achieve the Goals of the Five-Star System

CMS has several planned efforts intended to improve the Five-Star System. However, CMS has not taken steps to ensure that these efforts will help CMS achieve its goals for the Five-Star System—to inform consumers and improve provider quality. Specifically, CMS has not established intermediate goals and measures—such as interim milestones and related timelines—to guide the implementation of these efforts. In addition, CMS has not established how any changes resulting from these efforts, if implemented, will support the goals of the Five-Star System.

CMS Has Identified Efforts Intended to Improve the Five-Star System, but Lacks Milestones and Timelines to Guide Implementation

CMS has awarded contracts for or begun discussions about several planned efforts it has identified to improve the Five-Star System. These plans include evaluating its usability, adding information on nursing home capability, revising the staffing component, and developing additional quality measures. Specifically, CMS's planned efforts are:

- **To evaluate the usability of the _Nursing Home Compare_ website, which includes the Five-Star System**. CMS plans to conduct a multiphase evaluation of the usability of the _Nursing Home Compare_ website, which includes the Five-Star System, including testing the website with consumers and surveying stakeholders. In an effort to integrate the website with CMS's other "compare" websites, such as _Hospital Compare and Home Health Compare_, CMS is currently redesigning the website. As part of this redesign, CMS is changing the appearance of _Nursing Home Compare_ to be similar to that of other compare websites.[32] To inform this redesign, in December 2011, CMS tested proposed web page layouts for the revised website with a group of nine participants.[33] However, according to a senior CMS official, this testing and evaluation have been limited in scope and

---

[32]CMS anticipates launching the revised _Nursing Home Compare_ website in July 2012.

[33]Five of the participants were currently researching or had recently researched nursing homes for a family member and four participants were professionals who assist clients in finding nursing homes.

depth due to time constraints[34] and are only the first step toward gathering information on the usability of the *Nursing Home Compare* website and Five-Star System. The official stated that CMS plans to conduct a more in-depth evaluation of the *Nursing Home Compare* website and the Five-Star System than any done to date—one that includes more detailed consumer testing, a survey of long-term care stakeholders, and a web-based pop-up survey. CMS's Five-Star System contractor will assist with the more in-depth evaluation of the usability of the *Nursing Home Compare* website and the Five-Star System in fiscal year 2012.

- **To evaluate options to better distinguish among nursing homes' various care capabilities**. A senior CMS official stated that CMS is evaluating options for refining the *Nursing Home Compare* website and the Five-Star System to incorporate additional information about particular nursing home capabilities, such as whether a nursing home specializes in rehabilitative short-stay versus long-stay care.[35] One option is to post information on particular capabilities, such as whether a nursing home has a rehabilitation or dementia support unit. Another option under review is the creation of a rating system that assigns ratings separately for nursing homes that primarily provide short-stay care and for those that primarily provide long-stay care. In fiscal year 2012, CMS's Five-Star System contractor will develop options for additional information that might be collected regarding specific capabilities of nursing homes that would be useful to CMS or *Nursing Home Compare* and Five-Star System users.

- **To evaluate options to include other types of nursing home staff in the staffing component rating**. A senior CMS official stated that CMS would like to include some non-nurse staff, such as therapy

---

[34]CMS had September 2011 through early January 2012 to conduct evaluations and develop a proposal for the revised website so that the revisions could be incorporated and the revised website launched in July 2012. To prepare for the redesign, in October and November 2011, CMS also had contractors conduct an evaluation of the current website based on industry website design standards.

[35]Short-stay residents are those who typically enter a nursing home for a short period of time, such as after a hospitalization. In contrast, long-stay residents are those with chronic conditions who are typically long-term residents of a facility.

GAO-12-390 Five Star Quality Rating System

staff, in the staffing component of the Five-Star System.[36] However, CMS must first evaluate the feasibility and options for including additional staff. Subject to this evaluation, CMS officials said they would like to include some non-nursing staff in the staffing component by January 2013. CMS already collects data from nursing homes on some non-nursing staff levels, including therapy staff, but does not currently use this information to calculate the staffing rating.

- **To develop more quality measures for the quality measure component rating.** CMS is in the initial stages of identifying additional nursing home quality measures for use in the Five-Star System. CMS's Five-Star System contractor has been tasked with identifying potential measures for use in the Five-Star System in fiscal years 2011 and 2012.[37] A senior CMS official stated that identifying quality measures for the Five-Star System is an ongoing task under the contract and includes working with experts in the field of nursing home quality measure development, reviewing literature, and analyzing the results of potential quality measure data, such as data generated from MDS 3.0. In meetings with the technical expert panel, CMS and its contractor have solicited feedback from panel members on quality measures that would improve the Five-Star System.

Although CMS has several planned efforts intended to improve the Five-Star System, the agency has not established intermediate goals and measures—such as interim milestones and related timelines—that could be used to show progress or contribution towards implementing these efforts. Specifically, while CMS officials have given us broad estimates for

---

[36]The staffing component rating is based on the nursing staff levels (registered nurse, certified nursing assistant, and licensed practical nurse) at a nursing home. Therapy staff provide nursing home residents with rehabilitative services and may include occupational therapists, physical therapists, and speech/language pathologists.

[37]CMS also has a contract with another contractor to develop new nursing home quality measures, with a particular emphasis on measures for short-stay nursing home care. However, this contract is for the development of nursing home quality measures more broadly and is not specific to quality measures for use in the quality measure component of the Five-Star System. This contractor is also currently developing a new quality measure related to rehospitalizations of short-stay nursing home residents. It would measure the percentage of Medicare short-stay nursing home residents who, after being discharged from an acute care hospital, return to the hospital for any reason during their stay in the nursing home or within 30 days after discharge from the nursing home. CMS estimates that this quality measure will be finalized in the fall of 2012. Subsequently, CMS will consider this measure for use in the quality measure component of the Five-Star System.

when they anticipate some of these efforts to be undertaken, CMS does not have planning documents or strategies that outline specific milestones and timelines associated with implementing the agency's planned efforts to improve the Five-Star System. We have found, in our prior work, that developing and using specific milestones and timelines to guide and gauge progress toward achieving an agency's desired results is a leading practice for effective strategic planning and management.[38] Particularly because much of the implementation is to be conducted by the Five-Star System contractor, the use of milestones and timelines to guide and gauge implementation is especially useful for helping to ensure that CMS has clear expectations for its contractor and a means for determining whether appropriate progress has been made in implementing these efforts.

CMS Has Not Established How Its Planned Efforts Will Help Achieve Goals

CMS has not established, through planning activities or resulting planning documents, how its planned efforts to improve the Five-Star System will help CMS achieve the goals of the system—to inform consumers and improve provider quality. As a result, CMS may not be identifying and prioritizing its efforts in a manner that best ensures that the goals are being achieved. We have found, in our prior work, that aligning activities, resources, and goals is a leading strategic planning practice that can help agencies to more efficiently and effectively achieve their goals.[39]

CMS officials stated that the agency has no planning activities or resulting planning documents that link the Five-Star System's goals with CMS's efforts to improve the system and that establish priorities among the efforts, based on these goals. This lack of planning and priority setting may explain why CMS has taken limited steps to determine whether or to what extent the Five-Star System is achieving the primary goal of providing consumers with understandable and useful information on nursing home care. For example, consumer testing of the Five-Star System could provide information on the extent to which this goal is being achieved. According to AHRQ, consumer testing is a key practice for ensuring that health care quality information is publicly reported in a

---

[38]GAO/GGD/AIMD-99-69 and GAO/GGD-96-118.

[39]GAO/GGD-96-118 and GAO/GGD-97-180.

manner that is useful and understandable to consumers.[40] However, CMS has gathered very limited information from consumers regarding the usefulness of the Five-Star System[41] and it appears that CMS has not prioritized its efforts based on the goal of informing consumers.

In addition, CMS has not set specific priorities among its planned efforts based on how to best achieve the secondary goal of the Five-Star System—to improve provider quality. For example, while public reporting itself can be an incentive for providers to improve quality, there may be other efforts that could help CMS to further accomplish this goal. Nursing home quality measures serve a number of purposes, including providing data to nursing homes to help with their own quality improvement efforts. In addition, making quality measure information available to consumers allows them to distinguish among nursing homes' quality and provides an incentive for providers to improve their quality. Therefore, adding more individual quality measures to that rating component in the Five-Star System could potentially create even greater incentives as well as provide nursing homes with more data on how to improve the quality of their care. However, CMS has not explicitly prioritized this planned effort or others based on achievement of this secondary goal. This planning and prioritization is especially important for quality measures because quality measures can be costly and time intensive to develop, especially if new data need to be collected in order to create the measures.

---

[40]AHRQ has developed and disseminated best practices for the public reporting of health care quality information to consumers. AHRQ has reported that good consumer testing will not ask respondents if they understand the information presented, but rather, will ask them a knowledge question to determine if they are interpreting the information presented correctly. See S. Sofaer and J. Hibbard, *Best Practices in Public Reporting No. 2: Maximizing Consumer Understanding of Public Comparative Quality Reports: Effective Use of Explanatory Information,* AHRQ Publication No. 10-0082-1-EF (Rockville, Md.: Agency for Healthcare Research and Quality, June 2010) and S. Sofaer and J. Hibbard, *Best Practices in Public Reporting No.1: How to Effectively Present Health Care Performance Data to Consumers,* AHRQ Publication No.10-0082-2-EF (Rockville, Md.: Agency for Healthcare Research and Quality, June 2010).

[41]In the summer of 2009, CMS used a pop-up survey on its *Nursing Home Compare* website that included some questions related to the Five-Star System to gather very general reactions to the website. In addition, in November 2010, CMS asked participants in its Medicare Users Group—a focus group used by CMS to get early, high-level feedback on potential modifications to Medicare.gov—five questions regarding *Nursing Home Compare,* two of which focused on the Five-Star System. To date, CMS has not made any changes to the Five-Star System based on the information gathered.

CMS officials said that the agency has no planning activities or resulting planning documents related to the Five-Star System because there are too many intervening circumstances that make planning difficult. These include uncertainty about resources available for the Five-Star System due to competing resource needs within the agency, mandatory activities required by the Patient Protection and Affordable Care Act that take up staff time and effort, and other agency initiatives. However, CMS officials acknowledged that, as CMS's budget is more constrained, the development of planning documents that prioritize its efforts intended to improve the Five-Star System will become increasingly important.

Conclusions

In an attempt to make information on nursing home quality easier for consumers to understand and use, and to help improve provider quality, CMS developed and implemented the Five-Star System in 8 months using information that was readily available. This was a significant step toward increasing the transparency of information important to consumers, but for CMS to sustain the Five-Star System over time, the agency will need to continue making a concerted effort. CMS has made some efforts to update the Five-Star System as it reviews the system's underlying components to identify potential ways to improve the system over time. However, there can be significant challenges to ensuring that the Five-Star System remains useful and valid over time, especially when the components of that system continue to evolve. While CMS has identified efforts it intends to make to improve the Five-Star System, the agency has not strategically planned how to carry out these efforts, such as outlining the milestones and timelines that will help ensure that progress is being made. In addition, CMS has not clearly identified how each of its planned efforts will help achieve the goals of the Five-Star System. As a result, CMS may not know how it will prioritize and best leverage its available resources to implement these efforts and achieve the goals of the Five-Star System. Additionally, during this period of fiscal constraint, these strategic planning practices can help CMS to better anticipate and make resource allocation decisions that minimize the effect of funding constraints on accomplishing the goals of the Five-Star System.

Recommendations for Executive Action

In order to strengthen CMS's efforts to improve the Five-Star System, we recommend that the Administrator of CMS use strategic planning practices to:

- establish—through planning documents—how its planned efforts will help CMS achieve the goals of the Five-Star System, and

- develop milestones and timelines for each of its planned efforts.

Agency Comments

We received written comments on a draft of this report from HHS on behalf of CMS, which are reprinted in appendix III. CMS agreed with our recommendations and submitted general comments on the draft.

Specifically, CMS agreed with our recommendation to establish—through planning documents—how its planned efforts will help CMS achieve the goals of the Five-Star System. CMS stated that it will work to develop a strategic plan for the Five-Star System that will address the short- and long-term goals for the system and the manner in which those goals will be achieved. CMS said that it would include a mechanism for receiving regular input from consumers and other stakeholders as part of a strategic plan. CMS also agreed with our recommendation to develop milestones and timelines for each of its planned efforts. CMS acknowledged the importance of both a strategic plan and the use of specific timelines and milestones for measuring progress toward meeting the goals of the Five-Star System and budgeting for the resources needed to meet those goals.

We are sending copies of this report to the Secretary of HHS and the Administrator of CMS and other interested parties. In addition, the report also will be available at no charge on GAO's website at http://www.gao.gov.

If you or your staff members have any questions about this report, please contact me at (202) 512-7114 or kohnl@gao.gov. Contact points for our Offices of Congressional Relations and Public Affairs may be found on the last page of this report. Key contributors to this report are listed in appendix IV.

Linda T Kohn

Linda T. Kohn
Director, Health Care

Appendix I: Methodology for Identifying Key Methodological Decisions Made during Five-Star Quality Rating System Development

To identify the key methodological decisions made during the development of the Five-Star Quality Rating System (Five-Star System), defined as those that caused the most intense discussion and review according to at least six members of the Centers for Medicare & Medicaid Services' (CMS) technical expert panel, we solicited the views of panel members through a series of interviews and questionnaires.[1]

Specifically, we completed the following steps:

1. We interviewed each member of the technical expert panel using a structured interview set containing open-ended questions. During these interviews, we asked each member to provide their views on the top three methodological decisions that caused the most discussion and review during the development of the Five-Star System and to describe the differing views expressed by members of the panel on the methodological approach that CMS was considering.

2. We summarized the open-ended interview responses related to the views on the methodological decisions that caused the most discussion and review during the development of the Five-Star System.

3. We distributed a questionnaire to the members of the technical expert panel that outlined the methodological decisions identified during our interviews and asked each member to identify the six methodological decisions they recalled as eliciting the most intense review and discussion during the development of the Five-Star System.

4. We analyzed the responses to our questionnaire to identify the key methodological decisions—those that at least six members of CMS's technical expert panel recalled as eliciting the most intense review and discussion during the development of the Five-Star System. Seven of nine technical expert panel members responded to our questionnaire. We made multiple unsuccessful attempts to obtain completed questionnaires from the remaining two members over a 4 week period. (See table 1.)

---

[1]CMS convened a technical expert panel to provide recommendations on the development of the Five-Star System. This panel is composed of nine members that CMS and its contractor identified as experts in long-term care research and included researchers and an industry representative. For a list of the current technical expert panel, see https://www.cms.gov/CertificationandComplianc/13_FSQRS.asp.

Table 1: Key Methodological Decisions Made during the Development of the Five-Star System, as Identified by CMS's Technical Expert Panel

Methodological decisions	Key methodological decision[a]
Which information from surveys to use to calculate the ratings	
Which thresholds to use for assigning health inspection ratings[b]	
What staffing information, if any, to include in the rating system	
Whether and how to adjust staffing levels to reflect resident acuity[c]	X
How to combine the staffing measures to calculate the staffing ratings	
Which thresholds to use for assigning staffing ratings[b]	
Whether to exclude hospital-based facilities or set up separate staffing ratings for hospital-based and freestanding nursing homes[d]	
Which quality measures to include in the quality measure rating	
Whether and how to risk adjust the quality measures	
How to combine the individual measures to calculate the quality measure rating	
Which thresholds to use to assign quality measure ratings[b]	
Whether to create an overall rating	
How to combine the component ratings to create an overall rating	X
Which thresholds to use to assign an overall rating[b]	
Whether to exclude or set up separate overall ratings for hospital-based and freestanding nursing homes[d]	X

Source: GAO analysis of interviews with members of the technical expert panel that CMS convened to assist with the development of the Five-Star System.

[a]We defined key methodological decisions as those identified by six or more of the members of CMS's technical expert panel as eliciting the most intense review and discussion during the development of the Five-Star System.

[b]Thresholds refer to cut points above or below which nursing homes would be awarded a specific number of stars or points to be used to calculate star ratings.

[c]Resident acuity refers to the differences in the level of complexity of nursing services required to care for residents across nursing homes.

[d]Hospital-based nursing homes are under administrative control of a hospital. In contrast, freestanding nursing homes are those that are not under administrative control of a hospital.

Appendix II: Overview of CMS's Five-Star Quality Rating System Methodology

In the Five-Star System, nursing homes are assigned ratings for three components—health inspections, staffing, and quality measures—and an overall rating. These ratings range from one star to five stars, with more stars indicating higher quality.

Health Inspection Rating

Each nursing home is assigned a health inspection rating in comparison to other nursing homes in its state using a point system. These points are assigned based on the nursing home's three most recent health inspections—known as a survey—results, including survey revisits and complaint surveys, over the past 3 years.[1] Points are assigned based on the number, scope, and severity of a nursing home's health deficiencies found during surveys, with deficiencies with greater scope and severity equating to more points. Therefore, a lower survey point total results in a better rating (see table 2). If multiple revisits are required to ensure that major deficiencies are corrected, additional points are added to the health inspection score (see table 3). Based on the totals received, the top 10 percent of nursing homes in a given state receive five stars, the bottom 20 percent receive one star, and the middle 70 percent of nursing homes receive two, three or four stars, with equal proportions (23.33 percent) in each category.

---

[1]Points from more recent surveys are weighted more heavily. The most recent year's survey is assigned a weighing factor of 1/2, the previous survey has a weighing factor of 1/3, and the second prior survey has a weighing factor of 1/6.

Table 2: Health Inspection Score: Weights for Different Types of Deficiencies Identified in Nursing Homes

Severity	Scope		
	Isolated	Pattern	Widespread
Immediate jeopardy[a]	J 50 points[b] (75 points)	K 100 points[b] (125 points)	L 150 points[b] (175 points)
Actual harm	G 20 points	H 35 points (45 points)	I 45 points (50 points)
Potential for more than minimal harm	D 4 points	E 8 points	F 16 points (20 points)
Potential for minimal harm[c]	A 0 points	B 0 points	C 0 points

Source: CMS.

Note: Points are assigned to deficiencies based on the scope and severity of the deficiency and whether the deficiency constitutes substandard quality of care. Figures in parentheses indicate points for deficiencies that are for substandard quality of care. Deficiencies constitute substandard quality of care if they are cited at the scope/severity levels F or H through L because the nursing home did not meet a quality of care standard under the following federal regulations: 42 C.F.R § 483.13 (resident behavior and nursing home practices); 42 C.F.R § 483.15 (quality of life); 42 C.F.R § 483.25 (quality of care).

[a]Actual or potential for death/serious injury.

[b]If the status of the deficiency is identified as "past non-compliance" and the severity is Immediate Jeopardy, then points associated with a "G level" deficiency (i.e., 20 points) are assigned.

[c]Nursing home is considered to be in substantial compliance.

Table 3: Points Added to Health Inspection Score When Repeat Revisits Are Needed after a Health Inspection Survey Finds Deficiencies

Number of revisit surveys	Points
First	0
Second	50 percent of health inspection score
Third	70 percent of health inspection score
Fourth	85 percent of health inspection score

Source: CMS.

Staffing Rating

Each nursing home's staffing rating is calculated based on the facility's self-reported registered nurse (RN) and total nursing (sum of RN, licensed practical nurse, and certified nursing assistant) staffing levels for a 2-week period around the time a routine survey is conducted. Staffing levels are converted to hours per resident day and are adjusted to reflect varying levels of resident acuity.[2] Each nursing home's staffing rating is assigned based on how its total nursing and RN staffing levels compare to the distribution of staffing levels for freestanding facilities[3] in the nation and staffing level thresholds identified by CMS.[4] (See table 4.)

---

[2]Resident acuity refers to the complexity of nursing services required to care for residents, as measured using the Resource Utilization Group (RUG)-III case mix system. This system classifies residents into 1 of 53 categories according to predicted resource needs, particularly the expected amount of staff time required to care for residents, using resident assessment data that are routinely collected and reported to CMS by nursing homes using a resident assessment tool called the Minimum Data Set (MDS). Currently, resident acuity is measured using data from an older version of MDS that was collected through September 30, 2010. One CMS official told us that the agency anticipates beginning to use data from a new version of MDS to measure resident acuity beginning around April 2012.

[3]Freestanding nursing homes are those that are not under administrative control of a hospital. In contrast, hospital-based nursing homes are under administrative control of a hospital.

[4]See AM Kramer and R. Fish, Abt Associates, "The Relationship Between Nurse Staffing Levels and the Quality of Nursing Home Care," chapter 2 in *Appropriateness of Minimum Nurse Staffing Ratios in Nursing Homes: Phase II Final Report,* a report prepared at the request of CMS (2001).

Table 4: Scoring Method and Thresholds for Assigning Staffing Ratings in the Five-Star System

Star rating[a]	Definition	Range (adjusted hours per resident day)	Registered nurses Total nursing[b]
1	Less than 25th percentile[c]	<0.221	<2.998
2	At least 25th percentile but less than median[c]	≥0.221 – <0.298	≥2.998 – <3.376
3	Greater than or equal to the median but less the 75th percentile[c]	≥0.298 – <0.402	≥3.376 – <3.842
4	Greater than or equal to the 75th percentile[c]	≥0.402 – <0.550	≥3.842 – <4.080
5	At or exceeding the thresholds based on a 2001 CMS staffing study[d]	≥0.550	≥4.080

Source: CMS.

[a]CMS has developed an approach for assigning staffing ratings when ratings for registered nurse and total nursing staffing differ. See Centers for Medicare & Medicaid Services, *Design for Nursing Home Compare Five-Star Quality Rating System: Technical Users' Guide* (Baltimore, Md.: July 2010).

[b]Total nursing refers to the sum of registered nurses, licensed practical nurses, and certified nursing assistants.

[c]Each nursing home's staffing rating is assigned based on how its total nursing and registered nurse staffing levels compared to the distribution of staffing levels for freestanding facilities in the nation. The thresholds are based on the distribution of staffing data for freestanding facilities reported to CMS as of November 4, 2008.

[d]These thresholds are based on a 2001 CMS staffing study conducted to examine the levels at which nursing home staffing levels relate to improved quality of care. See AM Kramer and R. Fish, Abt Associates, "The Relationship Between Nurse Staffing Levels and the Quality of Nursing Home Care," chapter 2 in *Appropriateness of Minimum Nurse Staffing Ratios in Nursing Homes: Phase II Final Report*, a report prepared at the request of CMS (2001).

Quality Measure Rating

Each nursing home's quality measure rating is calculated based on the nursing home's performance over the three most recent quarters[5] on 10 of 19 quality measures,[6] including 7 long-stay and 3 short-stay measures.[7] Two of the long-stay measures capture aspects of activities of

[5]CMS has not updated the quality measure ratings in the Five-Star System since January 2011, while CMS collects resident information from nursing homes using the new version of MDS—MDS 3.0—which was implemented in October 2010 and refines and tests quality measures using this new assessment tool. CMS is currently considering options for how to refine the quality measure rating based on these new data.

[6]CMS selected these quality measures, with input from its Five-Star System contractor and members of a Five-Star System technical expert panel—a panel composed of nine individuals that CMS identified as experts in long-term care research—based on their validity and reliability, the extent to which the measure is under the facility's control, statistical performance, and importance.

[7]Short-stay measures are those that are intended to assess quality of care for residents who typically enter a nursing home for a short period, such as after a hospitalization. In contrast, long-stay measures are those that are intended to assess quality of care for residents with chronic conditions who are typically long-term residents of a facility.

daily living, which reflect nursing home residents' ability to provide self-care. Performance on the two activities of daily living-related measures is weighted 1.6667 times as high as the other measures. This, according to CMS, reflects the greater importance of these measures to many nursing home residents and ensures that the two activities of daily living measures count for 40 percent of the overall weight of the long-stay measures. For the individual quality measures used to calculate this rating, nursing homes that have lower percentages are considered to have higher quality of care and, thus, receive more points. For example, for one of the quality measures used in the Five-Star System—the percentage of patients who were physically restrained—nursing homes with lower percentages of patients who were physically restrained are considered to have higher quality of care. As a result, those nursing homes receive more points towards their quality measure rating than facilities in which a higher percentage of residents are physically restrained. The points received for all quality measures are summed to create a total score for each facility with a higher point total equating to a better quality measure star rating.[8] Quality measure ratings are then assigned to generally achieve the following distribution: the top 10 percent of nursing homes receive five stars, the bottom 20 percent receive one star, and the middle 70 percent of nursing homes receive two, three, or four stars, with equal proportions (23.33 percent) in each category.[9]

Overall Rating

Each nursing home's overall rating is based on its ratings for the three components—health inspections, staffing, and quality measures. From these three ratings, the overall rating is assigned based on the following steps:

1. Start with the number of stars for the health inspection rating.

---

[8]CMS has developed an approach for accounting for missing data for individual quality measures when calculating quality measure ratings. See Centers for Medicare & Medicaid Services, *Design for Nursing Home Compare Five-Star Quality Rating System: Technical Users' Guide* (Baltimore, Md.: 2010).

[9]Thresholds for the two activities of daily living quality measures are reset with each quarterly update of the quality measure data based on the state-specific distribution of these measures. Thresholds for the other quality measure ratings are fixed based on the national distribution of these measures on January 5, 2009.

2. Add one star if the staffing rating is four or five stars and also greater than the health inspection rating. Subtract one star if the staffing rating is one star. The rating cannot go above five stars or lower than one star.

3. Add one star if the quality measure rating is five stars. Subtract one star if the quality measure rating is one star. The rating cannot go above five stars or lower than one star.

If the health inspection rating is 1 star, then the overall rating cannot be upgraded by more than one star based on the staffing and quality measure ratings. In addition, if a nursing home is a Special Focus Facility[10] that has not graduated, the maximum overall rating allowable is 3 stars.

---

[10]The Special Focus Facility Program is a program that aims to remedy noncompliance with federal quality standards in nursing homes with repeated cycles of noncompliance with these standards. For additional information about this program, see GAO, *Nursing Homes: CMS's Special Focus Facility Methodology Should Better Target the Most Poorly Performing Homes, Which Tended to Be Chain Affiliated and For-Profit,* GAO-09-689 (Washington, D.C.: Aug. 28, 2009) and *Poorly Performing Nursing Homes: Special Focus Facilities Are Often Improving, but CMS's Program Could Be Strengthened,* GAO-10-197 (Washington, D.C.: Mar. 19, 2010).

Appendix III: Comments from the Department of Health and Human Services

DEPARTMENT OF HEALTH & HUMAN SERVICES   **OFFICE OF THE SECRETARY**

Assistant Secretary for Legislation
Washington, DC 20201

MAR 5 2012

Linda T. Kohn
Director, Health Care
U.S. Government Accountability Office
441 G Street NW
Washington, DC 20548

Dear Ms. Kohn:

Attached are comments on the U.S. Government Accountability Office's (GAO) report entitled,
"NURSING HOMES: CMS Needs Milestones and Timelines to Ensure Goals for the Five-Star
Quality Rating System Are Met" (GAO-12-390).

The Department appreciates the opportunity to review this draft section of the report prior to
publication.

Sincerely,

Jim R. Esquea
Assistant Secretary for Legislation

Attachment

**GENERAL COMMENTS OF THE DEPARTMENT OF HEALTH AND HUMAN
SERVICES (HHS) ON THE GOVERNMENT ACCOUNTABILITY OFFICE'S
(GAO) DRAFT REPORT ENTITLED, "NURSING HOMES: CMS NEEDS
MILESTONES AND TIMELINES TO ENSURE GOALS FOR THE FIVE-STAR
QUALITY RATING SYSTEM ARE MET" (GAO-12-390)**

In 2008 the Centers for Medicare & Medicaid Services (CMS) created the *Five Star
Nursing Home Quality Rating System* with broad input from stakeholders, researchers
and contract research firms. The GAO report notes that CMS has modified the *Five Star
Nursing Home Quality Rating System*, "in response to (1) methodological issues raised by
stakeholders, (2) its routine monitoring of the system, and (3) the availability of new data
sources."

The CMS is implementing additional improvements to the *Nursing Home Compare*
website. This includes new information about the number of substantiated complaints,
the result of CMS complaint investigations, monetary fines levied against nursing homes,
and new quality measures that will be possible as we complete the transition to reporting
on the new Minimum Data Set (MDS) 3.0. As noted in the report, in the future we intend
to add information about nursing home ownership and nursing homes' special
capabilities. These additions (and others are likely to emerge) suggest the need for a
more formal strategic plan for modifying the site and ensuring that the site meets CMS'
goal of informing consumers and improving provider quality.

The CMS developed *Nursing Home Compare* in 1998. The goal of *Nursing Home
Compare* was and remains to provide consumers with easily accessible and
understandable information that will allow consumers to make informed choices about
nursing homes. Since 1998, CMS has steadily expanded the site in response to
stakeholder input and its own analyses. In 1999, for example, CMS added information
about nursing home staffing. In 2001, CMS added the results of complaint surveys. In
2003, CMS began reporting quality measures for nursing homes. In 2007, CMS added
information about fire safety inspections and began identifying Special Focus Facilities.
And in 2008 CMS began publishing the *Five Star Nursing Home Quality Rating System*.

The significant expansion of information on *Nursing Home Compare* resulted in a very
complex website, a fact that a number of stakeholders, including members of Congress,
noted. For example, *Nursing Home Compare* reports the results of nearly 200,000
nursing home inspections and about 300,000 quality measure values. The *Five Star
Nursing Home Quality Rating System* therefore offers consumers a convenient way to
summarize the vast amount of information available on the website.

The report also notes that CMS has "several planned efforts intended to improve the
system the Five Star System" and recommends that CMS adopt "milestones and timelines
to guide and gauge progress toward achieving desired results and the alignment of
activities, resources, and goals."

<u>**GENERAL COMMENTS OF THE DEPARTMENT OF HEALTH AND HUMAN
SERVICES (HHS) ON THE GOVERNMENT ACCOUNTABILITY OFFICE'S
(GAO) DRAFT REPORT ENTITLED, "NURSING HOMES: CMS NEEDS
MILESTONES AND TIMELINES TO ENSURE GOALS FOR THE FIVE-STAR
QUALITY RATING SYSTEM ARE MET" (GAO-12-390)**</u>

The GAO also recommends that CMS more rigorously tie its "planned efforts to improve
the Five-Star system" to CMS' stated goals of informing consumers and improving
provider quality. CMS concurs fully with the GAO's findings and recommendation. The
GAO recommendations and the CMS response to those recommendations are discussed
below.

<u>**GAO Recommendation 1**</u>

In order to strengthen CMS's efforts to improve the Five-Star System, the GAO
recommends that the Administrator of CMS use strategic planning practices to
establish—through planning documents—how its planned efforts will help CMS achieve
the goals of the Five Star System.

<u>**CMS Response**</u>

The CMS concurs with this recommendation. CMS will work to develop a strategic plan
for *Nursing Home Compare and the Five Star System* that addresses CMS' short- and
long-term goals for the site and the ways in which CMS may best achieve those goals.
As part of this strategic plan, CMS will develop a mechanism for receiving regular and
systematic input from consumers, as well as from stakeholders.

<u>**GAO Recommendation 2**</u>

In order to strengthen CMS's efforts to improve the Five-Star System, the GAO
recommends that the Administrator of CMS use strategic planning practices to develop
milestones and timelines for each of its planned efforts.

<u>**CMS Response**</u>

The CMS concurs with this recommendation. Along with a strategic plan, we will
develop a timeline and milestones for meeting the CMS' goals. CMS acknowledges that
both the strategic plan and specific timelines and milestones are critical for—(1)
Measuring CMS' progress towards meeting its goals; and (2) Budgeting for the resources
needed to meet those goals.

The CMS appreciates the opportunity to comment on this draft report and we look
forward to working with GAO on this and other issues.

Appendix IV: GAO Contact and Staff Acknowledgments

GAO Contact	Linda Kohn, (202) 512-7114 or kohnl@gao.gov
Staff Acknowledgments	In addition to the contact named above, Karen Doran, Assistant Director; Danielle Bernstein; Deirdre Brown; Krister Friday; Giselle Hicks; Melanie Krause; Lisa Motley; and Jessica Smith made key contributions to this report.

GAO's Mission	The Government Accountability Office, the audit, evaluation, and investigative arm of Congress, exists to support Congress in meeting its constitutional responsibilities and to help improve the performance and accountability of the federal government for the American people. GAO examines the use of public funds; evaluates federal programs and policies; and provides analyses, recommendations, and other assistance to help Congress make informed oversight, policy, and funding decisions. GAO's commitment to good government is reflected in its core values of accountability, integrity, and reliability.
Obtaining Copies of GAO Reports and Testimony	The fastest and easiest way to obtain copies of GAO documents at no cost is through GAO's website (www.gao.gov). Each weekday afternoon, GAO posts on its website newly released reports, testimony, and correspondence. To have GAO e-mail you a list of newly posted products, go to www.gao.gov and select "E-mail Updates."
Order by Phone	The price of each GAO publication reflects GAO's actual cost of production and distribution and depends on the number of pages in the publication and whether the publication is printed in color or black and white. Pricing and ordering information is posted on GAO's website, http://www.gao.gov/ordering.htm. Place orders by calling (202) 512-6000, toll free (866) 801-7077, or TDD (202) 512-2537. Orders may be paid for using American Express, Discover Card, MasterCard, Visa, check, or money order. Call for additional information.
Connect with GAO	Connect with GAO on Facebook, Flickr, Twitter, and YouTube. Subscribe to our RSS Feeds or E-mail Updates. Listen to our Podcasts. Visit GAO on the web at www.gao.gov.
To Report Fraud, Waste, and Abuse in Federal Programs	Contact: Website: www.gao.gov/fraudnet/fraudnet.htm E-mail: fraudnet@gao.gov Automated answering system: (800) 424-5454 or (202) 512-7470
Congressional Relations	Katherine Siggerud, Managing Director, siggerudk@gao.gov, (202) 512-4400, U.S. Government Accountability Office, 441 G Street NW, Room 7125, Washington, DC 20548
Public Affairs	Chuck Young, Managing Director, youngc1@gao.gov, (202) 512-4800 U.S. Government Accountability Office, 441 G Street NW, Room 7149 Washington, DC 20548

Please Print on Recycled Paper.